Reflections

Finding Direction Through My Mind's Eye

A death-defying choice becomes a dynamic message of hope.

Reflections

Belleville, Ontario, Canada

REFLECTIONS

The sole intent of this book is for informational purposes only. If you are experiencing suicidal thoughts or know of someone who is at risk, please seek supportive intervention immediately by going to the hospital, contacting your doctor, emergency services, or crisis services in your area.

A portion of the sales of this book will go toward the Waterloo Region Suicide Prevention Council to support their ongoing efforts in suicide awareness.

Waterloo Region
Suicide Prevention Council

ISBN: 978-1-55452-714-4
LSI Edition: 978-1-55452-715-1

Cataloguing data available from Library and Archives Canada

To order additional copies, visit:
www.essencebookstore.com

For more information, please contact:
Cathy Read-Wilson
readwilson_cathy@yahoo.ca

Epic Press is an imprint of *Essence Publishing,* a Christian Book Publisher dedicated to furthering the work of Christ through the written word.
For more information, contact:

20 Hanna Court, Belleville, Ontario, Canada K8P 5J2
Phone: 1-800-238-6376 • Fax: (613) 962-3055
Email: info@essence-publishing.com
Web site: www.essence-publishing.com

Reflections

Finding Direction Through My Mind's Eye

A death-defying choice becomes a dynamic message of hope.

On July 7, 2010, I attempted suicide. In being given a second chance, I have vowed to do my best to help others facing the struggle of suicide-related behaviour. Where life was once more black than white, I now strive to find the kaleidoscope of colours that help keep faith, hope, and love in my mind's eye.

As we get older, it is expected we become wiser. Not so for me. At 45 years of age, depression descended on me. I was blindsided by a hurricane with my heart, mind, and soul caught in a whirlwind. My first rough period followed the death in November 2007 of a close friend, Susie. The photo to the right was taken two months before her death.

In July 2010, I once again fell prey to depression: this time, with near-fatal consequences. I wanted my life to end. I gave out no warning signs until a few hours prior to my suicide attempt. The act itself was spontaneous, but the thoughts were nothing new. Although I did in many ways want to live, I also wanted to be free of the internal pain that had plagued me over the years, including my youth.

Thankfully, I received life-saving intervention. Many others do not. It was only through the quick action of my counsellor, Theresa Karn, and the professional response of a 911 operator for Waterloo Regional Police, that I was given this second chance.

Creative Reflections

In October 2010, Thanksgiving Monday, I was re-directed to where I had been found in July. The sun was shining when I started down the path that day, but by the time I reached my "spot," it had started to rain; symbolism in the making.

Chris Eisenbraun speaks of rain drops as symbolic in a diametrical sense. Rain can be nourishing to the ground when not in overabundance; however, as in Japan in March 2011, when it comes in waves it can lead to a destructive end. "Life giving on one hand and potentially death dealing on the other."*

During that "thanks-giving" day, I took time to reflect and look at my surroundings. Through the lens of my camera, I found myself unconsciously exploring my reasons to live. My photography and my writing have since been a catalyst in my healing, resulting in this book.

To the many who have given me a helping and supportive hand—family, friends, social service networks, the individuals I have interacted with in my work at Self-Help Alliance, and Waterloo Region Crisis Services of the Canadian Mental Health Association—I dedicate this book.

* (www.scootermydaisyheads.com/fine_art/symbol_dictionary/rain.htm)

My Hope and Dream

I pray that those who are bound to the darkness and despair of life may one day thrive to seek the light in their dreams, as I continue to strive and seek for mine. The road to recovery is rough, but there are spots along the way where there is new pavement. The journey can and does get better, despite the potholes along the way.

We are all under construction.

Thanks to all my foremen and co-workers alike who helped me along my path! I cannot name everyone so therefore I will leave my thanks at that.

I would never wish a serious depression on anyone. Without the pivotal crisis I experienced, however, I would not be where I am today: embracing meaningful direction to my life. I hope that through my mind's eye, I can help others envision how serious an issue suicide is in our society, lessen the stigma associated with it, and at the same time, instil a sense of promise for life beyond those thoughts. It only takes one to break the silence. There is hope.

Speaking out can save lives!
Sincerely,

Cathy Read-Wilson

Down the path I dare to go.

What lies ahead I do not know.

Walking softly with uncertainty.

Beauty abounds, but blind to me.

Danger lurking just ahead,

I can't go on. I rest my head.

My worldview now all black, no white;

My inner rock has lost all fight.

A drop of hope, I hear a call.

Will I be found before I fall?

Some things in focus; some still not.

I see through cracks a battle to be fought.

A twist in fate and help on way.

I no longer want death to come this day.

A pillar of strength and fragility;

With a helping hand, I pray for stability.

Negative thoughts a danger are;

Now must stop before going too far.

Through faith, hope, and love, I see life's glow;
To follow my dream I now must go.

I would like to share a speech that my son, Jared, gave to his grade 8 class in April 2011. He was 13 at the time.

An example of his effort to heal and make sense of my behaviour.

Bullying and Depression: Through a 13-Year-Old's Eye

By Jared Wilson

Alright, I want you to imagine a boy that is in grade 9. He has been getting bullied for the past couple weeks, except for the past couple days, so he decides he is going to go home for lunch. As he is walking home, about halfway, he notices some kids following him. He ignores it, but when he stops to tie his shoes, they are on top of him hitting him and drawing on his face and stuff. When he gets home after school, his mom is home and she asks what happened. He lies because he figures that lying would be safest.

Later that night or week, he hears that his favourite relative is in a coma and they might pull the plug. He really wants to go but he can't because he has a big project due the next day and he has barely started. Now there is a teenager that is getting bullied, his favourite relative could die, and he is home alone. What does he do? Well he could either go talk to someone and express his feelings, or, he could suppress those feelings that, if they eventually come back, could lead to depression.

Today I'm going to take you down the path of him suppressing his feelings, the potential depression, and its effects on him, his friends and his family.

Many of you may know that this past summer I went through one of the scariest things possible. While I was at Canada's Wonderland my mother attempted suicide. Some of you may think "So what, she attempted suicide, that was awhile ago and now everything is back to normal." The reality is, if someone you know attempted suicide, you don't know how to act around them; if it's okay to leave them alone. Unfortunately for me, I have quite a bit of experience with people that have attempted suicide. As well as my mom, my sister once thought about suicide, and three other people that are related to me attempted, with one that died. But anyway, back on topic, the point is that depression is a serious thing and we can't ignore it. We need to talk about it.

First, I'll explain why someone could become depressed. Three possible things can occur: the least common and it is mostly for kids and teenagers—their parents get a divorce. The second is that they are getting bullied at school or even out of school. Lastly, a common thing is that someone close to them passed away.

Now, how many of you know how to spot someone who is depressed and what they'll act like? I can almost guarantee that you couldn't find all the people that are depressed because most of you probably think that only the so-called Emos* are depressed. When in reality, those are the only ones that can show that they are depressed without having their parents or friends be against them.

Some of the nicest people you could meet could actually be depressed. For example, one of the skaters on Canada's Olympic team was depressed. The easiest ones to spot are the ones that suddenly start wearing long sleeves, dark clothes, and joking around about dying or asking who would care if they died. The other ones, I'm not sure myself how to spot them. You just have to hope that they do something so you can tell before it's too late.

How many people here have either actually meant to bully someone or just done it as a joke? Well if it was just a joke, if the person you are doing it to doesn't know, they may think you mean it. If you do it every day, depending on if they have someone they can talk to or what their situation at home is like, they could either be alright with this joking, or head into serious trouble; they could become depressed. As well, what if they take their life due to bullying? Next time you go to make a joke, just remember that.

Alright, so now I have told you how to tell if someone is depressed, some of the reasons it could happen, and why bullying is such a big deal. So now I'll talk to you more about the [potential] effects of depression, which is basically suicide. Some people think that depression isn't a big deal, when the reality is that depression (if it gets bad enough and the person has no one to talk to) is just the beginning to a nightmare. Because the thing that comes after depression is usually the thoughts of suicide. Now whether or not the person goes through with these thoughts depends on who they have around them and who they talk to about it.

Now as I'm sure all of you know, suicide is a very big deal, and if someone in your family attempts or succeeds, it's never the same at your house, no matter how hard you try to get it back to normal. I'm not sure what is worse, having them attempt, or having them actually commit suicide. If you think about it, they are both terrifying because on one hand you have someone that attempted to kill themselves. So they were trying to take their life from you and since they didn't succeed you never know if you can leave them alone with out them attempting again. But the other side you have someone that actually succeeded on killing themselves and taking their life away from you. I'm not sure, it all depends on how you look at things, which one is worse.

For some of you, you might not care about what I'm talking about. But there is one thing I want you to take from this. I want you to be able to recognize the signs that someone you know is falling down the path of depression and tell someone. Who knows, you may even save their life.

So, if you end up in the same situation as the person I had you visualize at the beginning, please don't bury those feelings. Go talk to someone. As well, if you are someone that is bullying someone else, stop. You don't know what they are going through; for all you know their mom could have died. Even if that's not the case, don't bother because there's always the chance that it is the case.

Note that although some of the "terminology" may not be politically accurate, it was important to keep his message as intact as possible. Minor editing changes have been made without losing the intent of the message.

* ***Emo**, short for emotional, a music genre, and also a subculture of the 1990-2000s youth. This subculture has had the reputation of being depressed and prone to self-harmful activities. One study, however, has found this culture of youth to be rather supportive and encouraging of each other. Many of these kids face bullying challenges and are negatively labelled by other more "popular" youth.*

Ryalls, E.D. "Emo Subculture: An Examination of the Kids, Music and Style that Form Emo Subculture." Paper presented at the annual meeting of the NCA 93rd Annual Convention, TBA, Chicago, IL. <<www.allacademic.com/meta/p187580_index.html>>

Statistics

- Nearly 4,000 Canadians die each year by suicide, an average of 10 suicides per day.
- Canadians are about seven times more likely to die from suicide than to be the victim of a homicide.
- In 1998, suicide was the leading cause of death for men between the ages of 25-29 and 40-44; for women it was the leading cause of death for ages 30-34.
- For each death by suicide there are as many as 100 suicide attempts.
- 9,344 hospitalizations in Ontario were due to suicide attempts with an average length of stay of 6-7 days (2001-02 C.I.H.I).[1]
- Men represent the majority of suicide deaths in Canada and Ontario. Conversely, women comprise the majority of emergency department visits and hospitalizations for suicide attempts (MOHLTC, 2007).
- 83% of Canadians do not know that suicide is the leading cause of death among youth (Your Life Counts, National Poll: Harris/Decima, August 2010).
- Over 2.5 million Canadians know someone who has attempted or has died by suicide.[2]

[1] <<http://www.wrspc.ca/suicide-facts.html>>

[2] <<http://yourlifecounts.org/?p=345>>

CANADIAN MENTAL
HEALTH ASSOCIATION
Grand River Branch

Self Help Alliance
self help • peer support • recovery

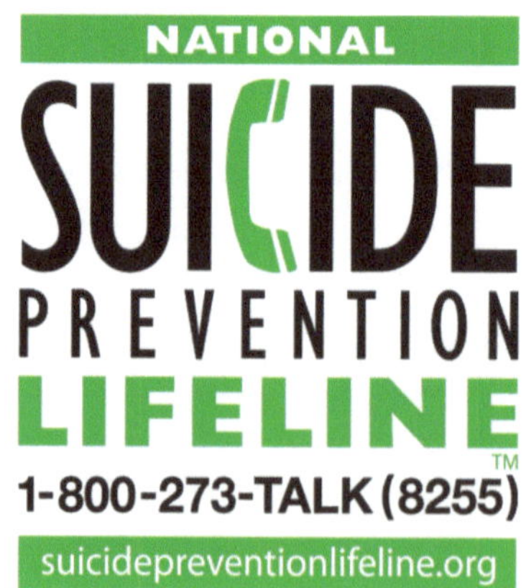
NATIONAL
SUICIDE
PREVENTION
LIFELINE
TM
1-800-273-TALK (8255)
suicidepreventionlifeline.org

www.ingramcontent.com/pod-product-compliance
Lightning Source LLC
Chambersburg PA
CBHW041223270326
41933CB00001B/27

* 9 7 8 1 5 5 4 5 2 7 1 5 1 *